Gray Wolf

By Dina Anastasio

Illustrated by Deny Bond

Modern Curriculum Press
Parsippany, New Jersey

ISBN 0-7652-2170-5

Printed in the United States of America

3 4 5 6 7 8 9 10   07 06 05 04 03 02

Modern
Curriculum
Press

Pearson Learning Group

1-800-321-3106
www.pearsonlearning.com

Contents

This book is for Eliza and Isabella.

The Wolf

Even though it was already spring, snow was falling. Late storms sometimes came to the mountains. They made it hard for the animals to find the food they needed.

The wolf was very hungry, but she knew that there would be no food today. Her pups were hungry too, but it was no use searching. By now all the rabbits and mice and squirrels had found places to hide from the snowstorm.

The wolf was called Gray Wolf. She was large and had thick gray fur. She was also still thin from living through the long winter with little food. The wolf could usually find at least one squirrel or rabbit for her pups to eat. Today she could not find any.

Her pups were not far away. Gray Wolf had left them in a hollow tree trunk where she knew they would be safe until she returned. She knew that her pups would not run away. The hollow tree was the only shelter the pups had ever known.

Gray Wolf's pups had been born six weeks ago at the beginning of March. They were still very young and needed their mother to do almost everything for them.

Gray Wolf sniffed the air. This storm was going to be a bad one. The wolf could not lie beside the fallen tree, near her pups, as she usually did. She needed to find a place out of the storm where they could all be together. She needed a place where she could keep warm, and where she could help her pups keep warm with the heat from her own body.

The snow was falling harder now. The biting wind was also turning colder. It froze Gray Wolf's damp fur coat and made her tremble, but she kept going. She would not stop until she reached her pups.

Gray Wolf remembered that the tree trunk was long and narrow and lying on its side on the ground. Now it was nearly covered with snow. She almost passed it before she smelled her pups inside.

The pups whimpered in their shelter. It was a soft whimper. They were too young to bark or howl.

Gray Wolf heard the pups and went toward them, making noises so that they would know she was there. When she had quieted them, she pushed her nose as far into the end of the tree trunk as she could. The pups came to her, one at a time. She licked them until they were warm again and they stopped whimpering.

The storm was now a blizzard. The wind was howling. It shook the trees so hard that branches broke. They snapped and cracked, falling around the wolf in the snow. The pups were whimpering again.

The pups must be moved quickly to a warmer place or they would freeze. Gray Wolf looked around. She remembered there was a small cave nearby. She had not gone to it before because humans were often there. Now she had to use it.

Gray Wolf left her pups again to search for the cave. She traveled in an ever widening circle away from the tree trunk, pushing her nose under bushes and between rocks.

When she finally saw the opening in the side of the rock face, she knew that she had found the right place. It was just deep enough to protect the wolves from the wind and snow. At the very back of the cave a drift of old leaves filled one corner. The leaves would make a nice bed and blanket for her pups.

The cave was not far from the tree trunk, but Gray Wolf had to hurry. She quickly returned to the tree and began to carry her pups one at a time in her mouth. One by one she put them down in the back of the small, dark cave. Then she pushed leaves over them to hide them and keep them warm.

Now only one pup, the smallest one, was still in the tree trunk. This pup was the runt. He was not as strong and healthy as his brothers and sisters.

All alone, the little one was frightened and cold. He had moved far back into the tree trunk to hide from the howling wind.

Gray Wolf tried to wiggle into the tree trunk. The small pup was too far back and the wolf was too big to fit. Gray Wolf grunted at the pup, but the pup would not come to her. He was warm in his little corner, and he was afraid of the storm. Gray Wolf shoved her paw into the tree trunk, trying to reach the pup, but still he would not come.

It took a long time to coax the pup to move. Finally he came out of the tree. Then he licked his mother's face and was glad to be carried like his brothers and sisters.

Gray Wolf almost had the smallest pup to the cave when her nose caught a new scent in the wind. It was a human scent. She trembled. Like all wolves, she was afraid of people.

Gray Wolf could not see the human, but her keen ears heard the soft, shushing sound of footsteps in the snow. Sometimes she heard the quick snap of branches cracking.

She stopped and listened. The pup she held by the loose skin on the back of his neck whimpered. The wolf shook him gently to quiet him. The human scent was strong, but Gray Wolf couldn't see much of anything in the blinding storm.

Chapter 2

Cally

Cally did not see the wolf as she hurried toward the cave. All she could see was snow. She was trying to reach the shelter in the rock face before the snow got too much deeper.

She did not hear the wolf either. All she could hear was the wind. It was blowing so hard that it was difficult to move, but she pushed on.

Cally called the cave her special thinking cave. She had been there many times before and knew exactly where it was. She had played there since she was a small child when she went to the mountains with her parents. It did not matter that the snow made it impossible to see. Cally's feet had followed that path so many times they could almost find the cave on their own.

In nice weather, Cally and her friends sometimes played in the cave every day. They would sit in a circle and make up stories like the stories their parents told them about their people and the way of the Native Americans. Her friend Richard often made up stories about a deer that had taken him high up into the mountains on its back. Maria sometimes made up stories about a giant turtle.

Cally made up stories about all kinds of things. One day she told her friends a story about a rabbit that could talk to humans. Another day she told them about a beautiful, singing butterfly.

Sometimes when it was raining, Cally and her friends sat by the cave opening and watched the raindrops for hours without saying a word. Then it was like being inside a waterfall.

Another reason Cally and her friends liked the cave was because it was dark inside. It was small but full of hidden nooks and corners. Sometimes the stories they made up were scary stories about what might be hiding in there.

Then it was fun to feel frightened. When Cally was with her friends it was different. Now she was all alone. This kind of frightened feeling was not fun at all.

Cally moved faster. She was brave, but she had
never been caught in a blizzard before. Today she
did not feel very brave. She was frightened. She was
all alone, and the wind seemed to be fighting her as
she struggled against it.

As she walked, Cally was becoming more and
more tired. Pushing through the snow was hard
work. She was beginning to daydream a little,
thinking about how nice it would be once she
reached the cave.

To help herself stop thinking about the snow, Cally began to think of all the happy times she had spent by herself in the cave while her mother looked for berries nearby. When she was alone in the cave, she would think about her ancestors who had roamed this mountain and had sat in this same cave hundreds of years before.

When she was there with her dog, Little Wind, she thought about all the animals and people who had come to the cave to get out of the rain or the snow or the wind. Maybe some had come there just to think, like Cally did.

Cally loved everything about her mountain. She loved the animals and birds that lived there. She loved picking summer flowers with her mother and the sound of a wolf howling far away.

Sometimes when Cally and her friends were
playing near the cave, a golden eagle would swoop
down over their heads. This frightened the other
children, especially when the huge bird soared
down to grab a small animal for dinner. It didn't
frighten Cally. She knew that many animals ate
other creatures in order to stay alive, and that was
the way of the world.

Cally could watch the eagle for hours as it soared
or hunted in the sky. Sometimes she would see it
land in the same place high on the mountaintop.
She knew that must be where the great bird made
its nest.

At home there were pictures of eagles hanging on
the walls of Cally's house. Her parents and her
grandparents said that the eagle ruled the skies.

Cally began thinking about Little Wind again. He loved the mountain and the cave as much as Cally did. She had named him Little Wind because he liked to race along the mountain paths.

Usually he did not run off alone, but today he had decided to chase a rabbit when he and Cally were out walking. Before Cally knew it, he was gone. Cally had followed him because she was afraid that he would get lost. She hadn't found him before the storm began. Then she had decided to go to the cave because it was closer than trying to get home.

Cally was worried about Little Wind. She had not heard him bark in a long time. She could not hear anything except the moaning of the wind. Maybe Little Wind was waiting for her in the cave. She had to reach it and find a way to keep warm.

The Cave

Cally was very tired when she finally reached the dark cave. She called for Little Wind, but she knew it was no use. If he had been near or in the cave, he would have barked when she got there.

Cally stamped the snow off her feet and rubbed her arms. She already felt warmer now that she was out of the wind and the snow.

The wind was blowing very hard, but she could hear the loud cry of an eagle nearby. She could tell by the sound that the eagle was after something, and she wondered what it was. The eagle cried again, and Cally stood up and moved to the opening, wondering if she would be able to see the bird.

The blizzard was fierce now, and it was hard to see anything except the white snow. She listened, but this time she did not hear the eagle. This time she heard a wolf's growl, and it too sounded very close.

Then Cally began to have a strange feeling that something was in the cave with her. She could not see or hear what it was.

"Hello?" she whispered softly. No one answered. The cave was silent.

"Is that you, Little Wind?" Cally asked hopefully.

Then she heard something. She was sure of it now. Someone or something was in the cave with her. It wasn't Little Wind because he would have barked and come to her. Who or what was it?

Cally tensed and waited. She was afraid to move. She wondered what it could be. She hoped it wasn't a bear that was hibernating in a corner of the cave. She was afraid of bears because a bear was the only animal on her mountain that would attack a human. Other animals, such as the wolf or the fox or the eagle, did not go after humans.

Cally turned and peered through the shadows of the cave. Slowly her eyes became used to the dark. Then she saw the four little wolf pups, and she knew that she would be all right.

Cally moved closer to see the pups better and sat
down to pet them. She was surprised and happy
when they didn't back away. Instead they crawled
into her lap and under her jacket. They cuddled
next to her because she was warm, and they were
cold and frightened.

The snow was falling so hard now that Cally knew she and the pups would have to spend the night in the cave. She wished that Little Wind was there with her. She was worried about him and hoped he was all right. She knew that her parents would be worried about her, too.

Cally left the pups back in their corner and went to the mouth of the cave. She could see the mother wolf now, a gray shape moving slowly through the snowdrifts. She could see that the wolf was carrying another pup in her mouth.

Cally knew that the wolf would be frightened when she saw a human. Cally was frightened, too. She knew that wolves almost never attacked humans, but what if the wolf thought Cally was harming her pups? Would she act differently then?

As Cally watched the wolf move toward the cave, she heard the eagle's cry again and understood what was going to happen. She had heard that cry many times before. The eagle had been forced out into the storm because it was hungry, too. Soon it might try to grab the pup that was in the wolf's mouth.

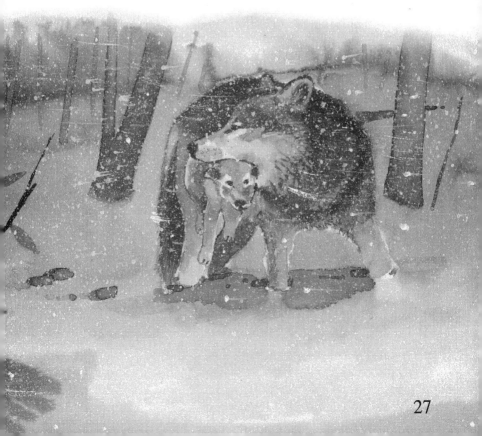

A full-grown golden eagle would probably be too large and too fast for the weary wolf. Its body, from the tip of its beak to the tip of its tail, was almost as long as Cally was tall. The wolf would have a hard time stopping a determined eagle from taking the little pup.

As Cally watched, she could see that the wolf was very tired. She was moving slowly toward the cave with the small pup hanging from her mouth.

"Hurry," Cally called to the wolf. "The eagle is coming. You must move faster." The wolf seemed to take no notice.

Cally tried again. "You have to run," she shouted over the roaring of the wind. "You have to run fast. Hurry!" Still the wolf did not run.

Then the eagle swooped down through the
swirling snow, just as Cally knew it would. It aimed
for the wolf, trying to grab the pup. The wolf
ducked, trying to shield the pup with her body.

Cally turned quickly and looked at the pups. They
were huddled together in their hiding place, in the
dry leaves at the back of the cave. They were
watching her. Cally had to do something to help
their mother.

Chapter 4

The Eagle

Gray Wolf saw movement in the corner of her eye. She whirled around just in time. She knew that the eagle was after her pup, and she was afraid.

As the eagle swooped down through the blinding snow, Gray Wolf lowered her head and crouched. The pup was beneath her now, so the huge bird could not snatch him with its sharp clawlike talons.

The bird flew up and down, trying again and again, but it was no use. After a while it gave up and soared back up into the sky. Gray Wolf hoped that the bird had gone away. She was so tired, she wasn't sure if she could defend her pup if the eagle attacked again.

Gray Wolf became aware that the human was calling. She was calling from the mouth of the cave, the cave where the other pups were. Gray Wolf did not know what to do.

Suddenly, the eagle came back. Gray Wolf heard its harsh cry. She knew that it was nearby, hovering in the sky. It was hidden by the snow, but it was there all the same. There was nothing for Gray Wolf to do but continue her journey toward the cave, even though the human was there.

She was almost to the cave entrance when the eagle swooped down again. The wolf felt the wind rushing down as the bird came closer, but she was too weak to fight. She lowered her head again to protect her pup and waited.

The giant bird landed and tried to steal the pup one more time, reaching for him with her talons. The wolf kept the pup under her chin where the eagle could not reach him.

The eagle rose up in the air, then swooped down one last time. It soared down, ready to snatch the little pup away.

Gray Wolf did not flinch. The eagle's claws could not grab the pup. One giant wing grazed the wolf's icy fur as the eagle rose up once more and flew back to take shelter in a tree.

Gray Wolf trembled. The eagle had come so close to stealing the pup away from her. She would do anything to keep her tiny pup safe. The cold and her hunger had weakened her, though, and she might not be able to withstand another attack.

After the eagle left, Gray Wolf lowered her body to the ground and lay there, waiting. The wolf did not know why the eagle did not come again, but she was glad for it.

She stayed on the ground with the pup beneath her and listened to the wind howl. She caught the scent of the human and was afraid, but there was nothing she could do. She had no strength left.

Then the wolf heard something. She looked up. She saw the human standing at the entrance of the cave. She was holding one of the pups. The pup was licking her face.

The wolf was frightened enough for her pups to make one last effort. She pulled herself to her feet and moved toward the cave with the smallest pup still in her mouth.

After Gray Wolf came into the cave, the girl put down the pup she held. The wolf gathered all of her pups together in the back of the cave.

The pups were all there, every single one. Gray Wolf was happy to see them. She licked them gently. Then she lay down on the floor of the cave and moved them closer to her body so that they would be warm. She could feel the girl there beside her.

The Wolf Pups

Cally stood near the wolves and watched them. The little one seemed very weak, and Cally was worried about him. All the wolves needed food. Cally tried to think of something that she could do. Then she remembered! There was food in the cave.

A few days before, Cally and Little Wind had
been playing in the cave. Cally had some dog
biscuits in her pocket, and Little Wind wouldn't
leave her alone. He kept trying to get at the biscuits
in Cally's pocket. So she had given him one and
hidden the rest way up high in the back of the cave.
Were they still there? Cally wondered if wolves
liked dog biscuits.

Slowly, she moved to the back of the cave. She
was careful not to come too close to the wolf
because she didn't want to frighten her. The gray
wolf watched her but did not move. Cally could see
that she was too tired to do anything but lie there.

She felt along the ledge and found the biscuits.
She placed them in front of the wolves. Then she sat
down on the other side of the cave. She waited to
see what the wolves would do.

The biggest pup found the biscuits first. He
sniffed them. Then he licked one and ate it. When
the mother wolf saw that, she took a biscuit in her
mouth and gave it to the little weak pup.

The little pup ate the biscuit. Then all the pups
ate some, crunching the biscuits just like Little Wind
liked to do. Cally listened to the crunch and smiled.
At least the wolves had something to eat.

The blizzard still raged outside the cave, and Cally was cold. She was glad that the wolves were there with her. If she had been all alone she would have been very scared. She didn't feel as frightened with the wolves there.

Cally started to talk to the wolves as if they were her friends. She pretended that they were all in a circle and it was her turn to tell a story.

"I feel better now that you are here," she said, "but my parents must be very worried about me. They might be searching for me now. If they find us, they will give us food, and that will make us all feel better. Maybe the storm is too bad for them to search, and they'll have to wait until the snow stops. Maybe they won't find us until morning."

Cally was beginning to feel frightened again. She was sleepy too, and very hungry. She tried to think about the wolves because that would make her forget how hungry she was.

Outside the cave it was getting dark. The weather was so bad that Cally knew the search party would have to wait until morning. She began thinking about her ancestors again and about the wolves' ancestors, too.

"Do you think that our ancestors sat here together a long time ago?" she asked the wolves. "Do you think that thousands of years ago there was a storm, and other wolves and other people sat together in this cave like we are doing?" On the other side of the cave, the wolves were silent.

After a while, Cally fell asleep. She dreamed of
wolf pups and Little Wind. It was summer in the
dream, and they were playing hide-and-seek
together. Little Wind was hiding so well that no one
could find him. In the dream the pups were calling
his name.

"Come out, Little Wind," they called. "It's time to
come out."

When Cally woke she felt very warm. At first she
thought that it was summer and she was playing
hide-and-seek because that was what she had been
dreaming.

Then she remembered. She was in a cave with a wolf and five pups, and there was a big snowstorm outside. She wondered if it was morning yet. She rubbed her eyes and tried to see, but it was dark in the cave. She was warm, almost hot, so maybe the storm had passed, she thought.

Then she realized it was the wolves that were making her so warm. While Cally had slept, the wolf had pulled the pups beside Cally and then lay next to her too, so they could all stay warm. She could feel the pups wriggling against her arms and legs. It made her smile.

The pups were whimpering again. Cally knew it was because they were hungry again. She was hungry, too. If the snow had stopped, she could go out and try to find food for all of them.

Cally pushed the wolf and the pups aside gently and stood up. It was strangely dark and quiet in the cave. Then Cally realized they were snowed in. During the night it had snowed so much that the entrance to the cave had been completely covered.

Cally had heard stories about this happening, and she knew they were in danger. If the opening was covered, air could not get in. Soon they would not be able to breathe. They had to get out of there!

Working Together

Gray Wolf was worried about the smallest pup. He didn't seem to be breathing well and she wondered why. The other pups seemed weak, but the wolf knew that was because they were so hungry. The littlest pup had something worse than hunger.

The wolf began to whine, and the girl came to her. She looked at the little pup, and then she placed her hand on the wolf's back. Gray Wolf became quiet then as she looked up at the girl.

The girl moved to the front of the cave and began to dig at the snow with her hands. Gray Wolf watched her. She used her snout to nudge her pups together. Then she went to the girl.

The wolf began to dig alongside the girl. She used her sharp claws to scratch and pull at the snow. She was very weak and very hungry, but she did not stop digging.

Side by side, the wolf and the girl scraped at the snow. The girl used her fingers, and as the snow broke up she grabbed chunks of it and tossed them behind her. They dug quickly, gasping for breath, until they had opened a hole. The fresh air that came in felt good.

The girl sucked at the air again and again with great gulping breaths. Then, one by one, she carried the pups to the opening while the wolf took deep breaths. The littlest pup was first. The air seemed to help. The pup began to breathe normally.

When they had rested, Gray Wolf and the girl began to dig again. Now Gray Wolf knew there was fresh air and sunshine on the other side of the snow. The great storm had ended.

After they had dug a long time, the hole was finally big enough for the wolf to climb through. When she was on the other side, she sat and waited. The girl took the pups, one by one. She pushed them through to Gray Wolf. When they were all out, Gray Wolf waited for the girl to crawl out, too.

Just as the girl was about to come out, something happened. The snow collapsed and fell, and the hole disappeared. The girl was still inside the dark place. Gray Wolf wanted to help her, but she needed to take care of her pups. The littlest pup was still very weak.

Gray Wolf picked up the first pup and ran. Even though the heavy snow had covered everything, Gray Wolf wanted to find the tree trunk. The snow on the path was deep, but the wind had blown the snow to the side so it was not as deep as the snow on either side.

Gray Wolf carefully followed this narrow trail. When she reached the fallen tree, she found it covered with snow. She put down the pup and dug at one end of the tree with her paws until she had uncovered the opening. When her pup was safely inside, she went back for another and another. She carried them quickly, one at a time, until they were all safely inside.

Even though Gray Wolf hurried, it took a long time. While she carried her pups, she wondered what would happen to the girl that was still inside the cave.

Snowbound

Inside the dark cave, Cally rested. In a minute she would get up and start to dig again. She had been digging at the snow all by herself for a long time. She was very tired, but she couldn't rest for long. The snow covering the opening meant that soon there would be no air.

Cally remembered the bright sun and glittering snow she had seen through the hole. She remembered the fresh air and how strong it made her feel. She began to dig again.

Cally was glad the wolf and her pups had gotten away. She hoped they were having a nice breakfast after their long, hungry night in the cave. Cally was hungry, too.

As she dug at the snow, Cally began to think about food. She imagined a big stack of pancakes dripping with syrup. She imagined crunchy toast thickly spread with butter. She even thought she could hear the crunching sound it would make.

She stopped. There really was a crunching sound. Something was scratching at the snow that blocked the entrance of the cave.

Cally wondered what was scratching out there. Maybe it was her parents, looking for her.

She called out, "It's me, Cally. Help me."

There was no answer. Cally knew that if there were other people out there, they would call back to her. If it was Little Wind, he would have barked.

Maybe it was a bear. Cally hoped someone from her village would find her soon. A search party would frighten away the bear. A group of many people could quickly dig her out of the cave.

Cally was trying to decide if she should keep digging when she heard the wolf. She was growling and whining outside the cave. Cally wondered if she was growling at the bear. Maybe the wolf would chase the bear away.

Cally started to dig quickly. As she dug, she heard more scratching and the sound of the wolf's whining. The whining was so loud that it sounded like it was right next to her. Suddenly there was light coming through the entrance. It was just a little light at first, and then more and more as she dug harder and the scratching continued from the other side.

When the opening was finally big enough, she saw the wolf. She was sitting at the other side of the tunnel they had just dug together. She was watching Cally.

Cally sat on her heels and stared back at the wolf
through the hole. They sat there for what seemed like
a long time, watching each other. Now Cally knew
that the scratching had been the wolf. The wolf had
been helping her escape.

"Thank you," she whispered to the wolf.

Then the wolf pushed through the hole. She took Cally's jacket in her teeth and pulled her toward the opening. Cally took a deep breath and climbed through the hole that she and the wolf had dug together.

When she was outside, Cally breathed great gulps of air again and again. Then she cried. She cried because she was so tired and so hungry.

While Cally rested, the wolf went to the tree trunk and checked on her pups. Then she went back to Cally.

The snow was too deep for Cally to walk home. She had tried, but she had only made it a few feet before she ended up getting stuck. So she had to wait for someone from her village to find her. She hoped someone came soon.

Cally and the wolf huddled together, keeping each other warm in the cold, deep snow. Cally wondered why the wolf did not leave her, but she was glad not to be alone.

Suddenly Cally heard barking, first from far off and then growing nearer and nearer. It was Little Wind! Because he was small, it was easy for him to run on top of the snow. He must have caught Cally's scent because he barked and barked all the way up the path until Cally could see him. Then he stopped, whimpered, and ran away.

"What's the matter, Little Wind?" Cally called after him. "What are you afraid of? It's me, Cally. I won't hurt you."

Then Cally remembered the wolf. That was it. Little Wind was afraid of the wolf.

"Don't be frightened," Cally called again. "The wolf won't hurt you."

Little Wind did not come back. Cally and the wolf were all alone again. Cally began to wonder if anyone but Little Wind was looking for her.

The Rescue

Cally would be surprised at how many people were out searching for her. They were making their way up the mountain, wearing wide snowshoes that kept them from sinking into the deep snow and getting stuck.

Cally's father led the search party. They fought against the deep snow and the steep mountain. It was hard work. Sometimes snowdrifts fell and blocked their way.

When the search party got closer, Cally could hear them. She had nearly fallen asleep, one arm across the quiet wolf's warm, furry back.

"I'm here," she called, but her voice was weak. "I'm here," she called again. She heard her father's voice shout in answer. "I'm OK," she called, louder now.

She felt the wolf wiggle away from her. Then in a few moments, Cally was being hugged in strong arms. "Your mother and I have been so worried," her father told her. "We started out for the cave as soon as it was daybreak. I knew you would hide there if you could."

He went over and touched the edges of the hole Cally had been pulled through. "I see you had to dig your way out of that cave. You must have been very frightened," he said.

"I didn't dig my way out of the cave," Cally said. "My friend dug me out."

Cally's father looked puzzled. There was no one there but Cally. The wolf had gone to hide as soon as she had heard the search party. Cally looked around, hoping the wolf had not gone far.

Cally took her father's hand and led him toward a boulder next to the rock face. The wolf was waiting behind it, out of sight of the humans. She was wary, but she seemed to be waiting for something.

"This is my new friend," Cally told her father. "The wolf saved my life. She dug the tunnel in the snow. When the snow covered the entrance to the cave, there was no air. I couldn't breathe, and the wolf saved me. When I was cold in the cave, the wolf kept me warm. She needs food for her pups."

"All right," her father said, "let's see what we can do." Cally and her father went with the search party back down the mountain to her village. The wolf followed a safe distance behind. Cally was sure the wolf knew they were going to help her and her five pups.

Before Cally reached her home, her mother ran out to hug her. Cally and her father told her about the wolf. Cally's mother went inside and came back with some meat she had been planning to cook for dinner that night.

Cally unwrapped the meat and put it on the ground near the wolf. The wolf looked at Cally for a long time. Then she took the meat in her mouth and turned to go back up the mountain. Cally knew she was taking the meat back to her pups.

Cally's mother gave her warm, dry clothes that had been waiting by the fire. Then Cally drank three bowls of steaming soup while Little Wind sat beside her and wagged his tail. Back on the mountain it had felt as if she'd be cold forever, but now Cally felt warm and safe.

That was the very last storm of the winter that had not wanted to go away. Afterward the warm spring weather finally came to the mountain. Cally and Little Wind went to the cave again. Once or twice they saw the golden eagle soaring high in the air, but there was no sign of the friend that had saved Cally's life.

Spring turned to summer and then to fall, and still Cally did not see the wolf. Then one night in December, Cally saw her. The winter storms had returned, and Cally heard her howling. She opened her back door and the wolf was there, watching her. Cally knew why the wolf was there. She was hungry and remembered how Cally had helped her before. Once again, Cally gave meat to the wolf.

That was the last time Cally saw the wolf.
Sometimes she still heard her, though, out in the
night, howling at something that Cally could not
see. She knew it was her wolf. The howl was part of
Cally now, like the sound of the wind or the cry of
the golden eagle. She knew it as well as she knew
Little Wind's bark. Whenever she heard the wolf's
howl, she thought of the night in the cave, and it
made her smile.

Glossary

ancestors (AN ses turz) relatives who lived long ago

blizzard (BLIHZ urd) a blinding snowstorm with a very strong wind

coax (kohks) to try to get someone to do something

determined (dee TUR mund) made up one's mind to do something

hibernating (HYE bur nayt ihng) spending the winter in an inactive state like sleep

huddled (HUD uld) crowded close together

runt (runt) animal that is smaller than the usual size

swoop (swoop) come down with a rush

talons (TAL unz) claws of an animal, especially those of a hunting bird

tremble (TREM bul) shake because of fear, weakness, or cold